Millie Marotta's
Woodland Wild

a colouring book adventure

BATSFORD

Introduction

Woodlands are wondrous places. For me they evoke a sense of adventure and exploration, conjuring memories of a childhood spent playing in the forests of mid-Wales. Spending time among the trees can allow us to feel a real connection with nature, with all the sounds and colours, the smell of moss on the forest floor, the dappled sunlight, the cacophony of the dawn chorus or the stirring rustle of leaves in the wind. Woodlands can be soothing and tranquil, somewhere to escape from the hustle and bustle, or they can be noisy and raucous, alive with shrill birdsong and buzzing insects.

Our woods are essential for life on earth, providing food, medicine and fresh water; they even give us the very air we breathe by sucking up carbon dioxide and releasing oxygen. And while many people work tirelessly to protect them, they remain under increasing threat as do the animals that live there. And so this book is about championing our magnificent arboreal habitats across the world and the marvellous animals that call them home.

Woodlands come in many forms, from the statuesque pines of Russia, to the humid canopies of the tropical rainforest. They are home to 80 percent of Earth's land animals and plants – vibrant, bold and alive with colour. What better theme for a colouring book?

Enter a realm of towering trees, howling wolves and slithering snakes, leafy canopies, underground burrows, soothing birdsong and busy insects. *Woodland Wild* is a celebration of the world's woodlands in all their colourful glory, although I have been able to feature only a tiny fraction of the species that thrive in our forested habitats. As trees are found in all corners of the globe (except Antarctica), the book features a huge variety of species from every continent. Some you will

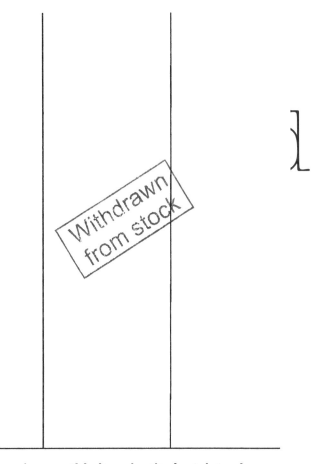

Please return/renew this item by the last date shown.

Herefordshire
Libraries

 **Herefordshire**
Council

First published in the United Kingdom in 2020 by
Batsford
43 Great Ormond Street
London
WC1N 3HZ
United Kingdom

An imprint of Pavilion Books Group Ltd

Illustrations copyright © Millie Marotta Ltd, 2020
Volume copyright © Batsford, 2020

ISBN: 9781849946421

A CIP catalogue record for this book is available
from the British Library.

30 29 28 27 26 25 24 23 22 21 20
10 9 8 7 6 5 4 3 2 1

Reproduction by Mission Ltd, Hong Kong
Printed by 1010 Printing International Ltd, China

This book can be ordered direct from the publisher at the website:
www.pavilionbooks.com, or try your local bookshop.

recognize, such as the cunning fox or the exquisite goldfinch, found in our own British woodlands, while others are a little more unusual and may be new to you, like the mystical saola from Southeast Asia or the Christmas Island crabs, who emerge in their millions, marching across the forest floor, making their way to the ocean to breed.

And when it comes to colour, there's no better artist than Mother Nature. So, whether your preferred palette is luminous greens, candy pinks, eye-popping fluorescents, or perhaps harmonious hues, *Woodland Wild* offers a kaleidoscope of colourful choices. From the Indian giant squirrel to the Guyana toucanet, the Bengal tiger of India to the feather-horned beetle of Australia, I hope the book will surprise and delight you as you weave your way through its pages.

For those of you who like to know exactly what species you're colouring, there's a glossary at the back of the book, and while this is a colouring book first and foremost, I love the thought that it might also offer you the chance to learn more about our animal kingdom.

And for those among you who enjoy practising your drawing skills as well as your colouring, there's a scattering of pages throughout the book that have been left less detailed than the rest, inviting you not only to bring them to life with colour but to embellish and decorate to your heart's content. Don't forget the tester pages at the back, where you can try out your colour combinations or test your materials, before committing to your colouring page.

The variety of colour combinations, techniques and materials used in the coloured illustrations gracing the walls of my online gallery and on social media are simply astounding, and as colourists across the globe continue to share their creations I'm still in awe, eight books later, at the wonderful community we have formed and the individuality of the images you create. My illustrations are just a starting point — you are the ones who bring them to life as your very own masterpieces. Making these books is rather a self-indulgent pursuit — I feel very lucky that I get to combine my two great passions, drawing and nature, and I love seeing how colouring and being creative can make people feel happy.

I cannot wait to see your *Woodland Wild* come to life. Whether you like to colour alone, with family and friends, use it as a creative outlet, or for mindful relaxation, I hope you will enjoy flooding these pages with colour as much as I enjoyed making the book.

So, crack open those colours — let the woodland adventure begin.

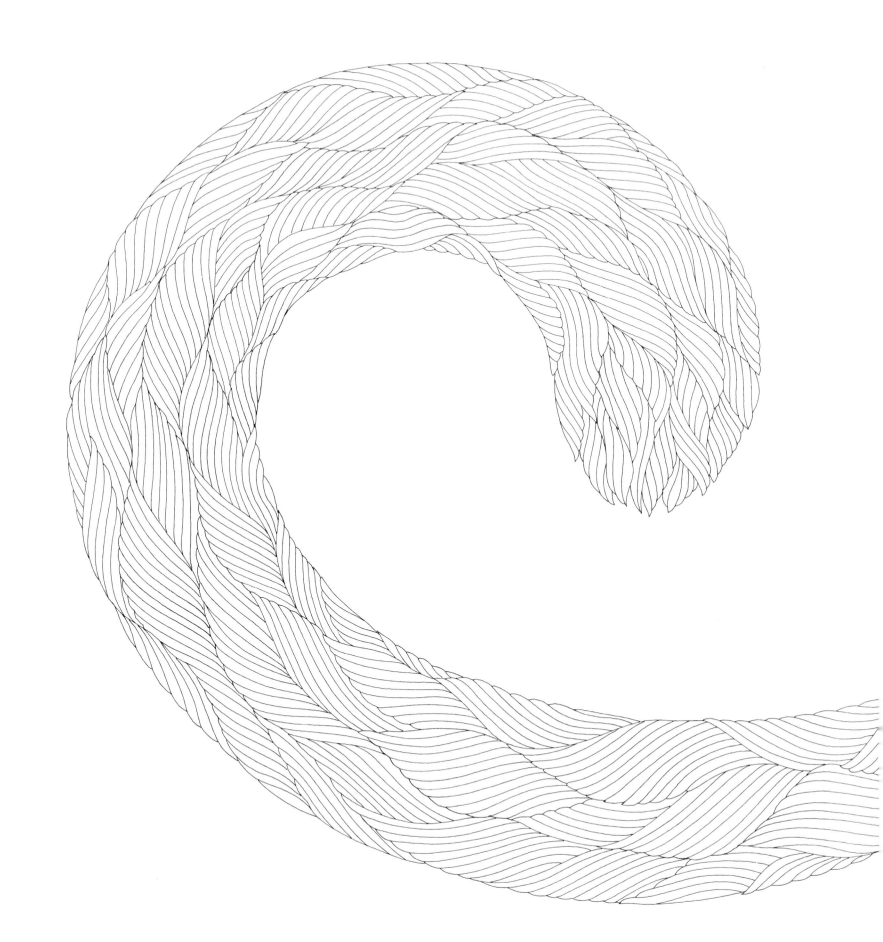

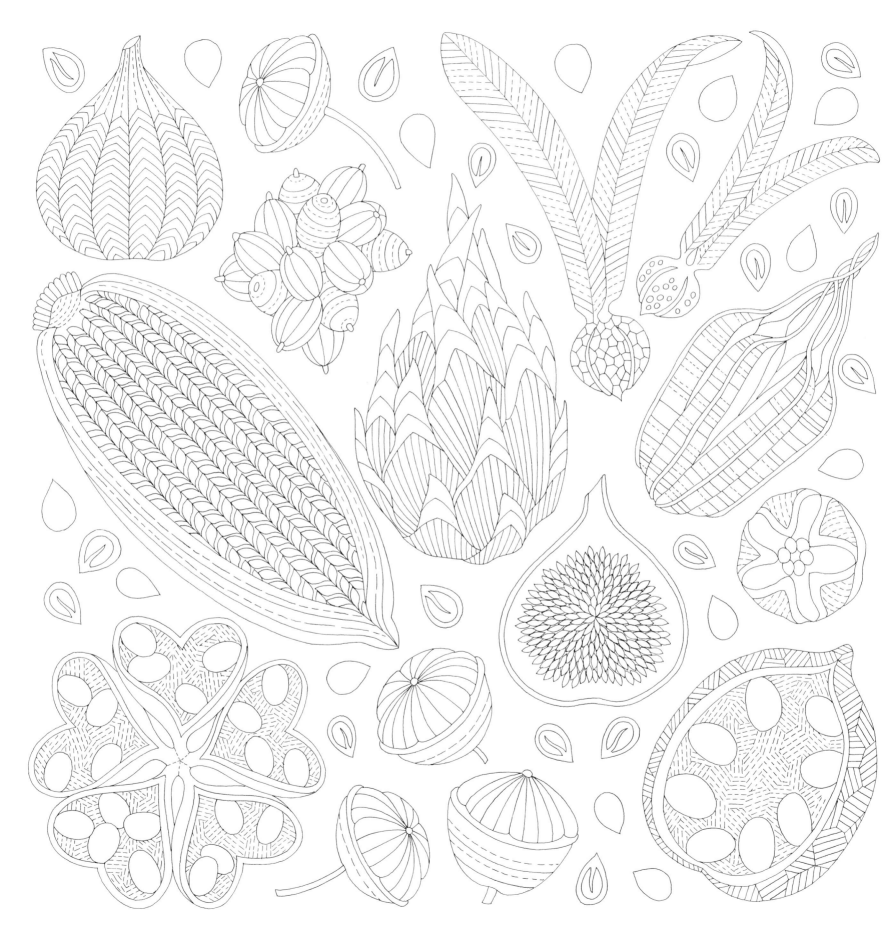

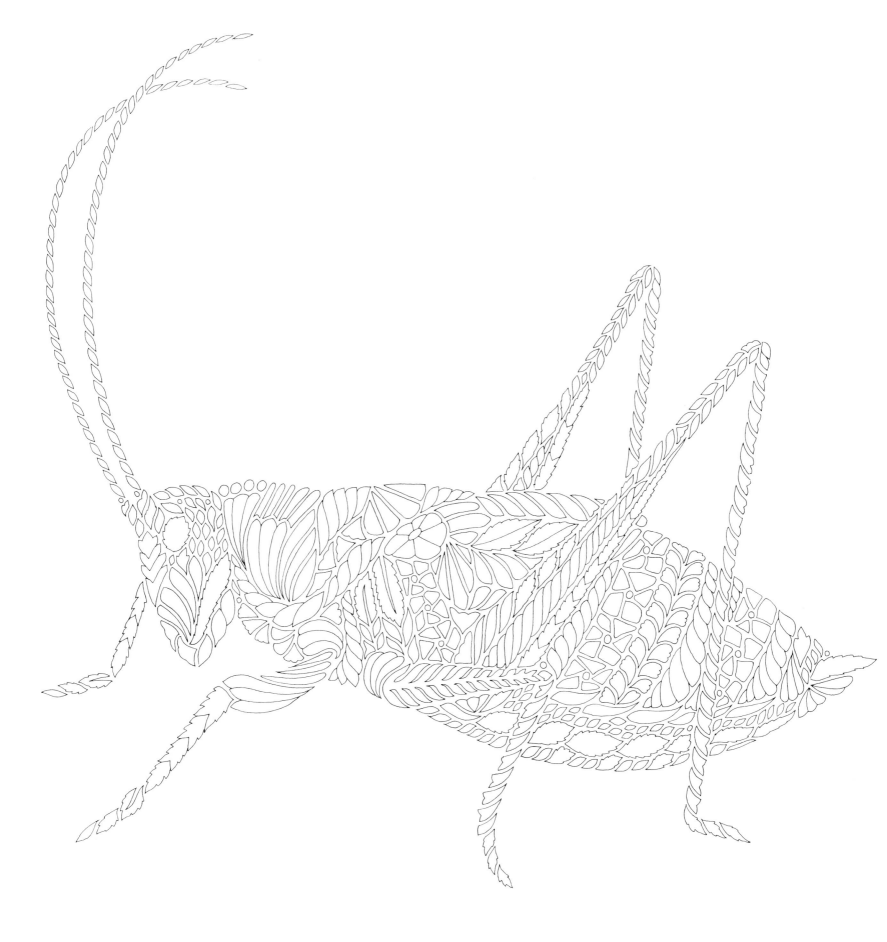

List of creatures in *Woodland Wild*

In order of appearance:

European rabbit (*Oryctolagus cuniculus*)

Fallow deer (*Dama dama*)

Japanese pygmy woodpecker
(*Yungipicus kizuki*)

Indian peafowl (*Pavo cristatus*)

European badger (*Meles meles*)

Ginkgo (*Ginkgo biloba*)

European adder (*Vipera berus*)

Eastern spinebill
(*Acanthorhynchus tenuirostris*)

Ferns
Hartford fern (*Lygodium palmatum*)
Maidenhair fern (*Adiantum
raddianum*)
Curly grass fern (*Schizaea pusilla*)
Toothbrush fern
(*Schizaea pectinata*)

Eurasian wren (*Troglodytes troglodytes*)

Red fox (*Vulpes vulpes*)

Fireflies (*Photinus carolinus*)

Indian giant squirrel (*Ratufa indica*)

Rosalia longicorn beetle
(*Rosalia alpina*)

European goldfinches
(*Carduelis carduelis*) and
hazel catkins (*Corylus avellana*)

Merveille du jour moth
(*Moma alpium*)

Wild berries
Juniper (*Juniperus communis*)
Holly (*Ilex aquifolium*)
European spindle
(*Euonymus europaeus*)
Sloe (*Prunus spinosa*)
Hawthorn (*Crataegus monogyna*)
Wild strawberries (*Fragaria vesca*)

European polecat (*Mustela putorius*)

Woodland flowers
Dunsborough donkey orchid
(*Diuris jonesii*)
Wood anemone (*Anemone nemorosa*)
Jack-in-the-pulpit
(*Arisaema triphyllum*)
Eastern red columbine
(*Aquilegia canadensis*)
Passionflower (*Passiflora caerulea*)
Cowslip (*Primula veris*)

Little owl (*Athene noctua*)

Common fig (*Ficus carica*)

Tropical seeds and fruits
Common fig (*Ficus carica*)
Coffee (*Coffea arabica*)
Dragonfruit (*Hylocereus undatus*)
Dutchmans' pipe seed pod
(*Aristolochia macrophylla*)
Manuka seed pod
(*Leptospermum scoparium*)

Peanut tree seed pod
(*Sterculia quadrifida*)

Ivory cane palm (*Pinanga coronata*)

Sal tree seed pod (*Shorea robusta*)

O'ahu tree snail (*Achatinella mustelina*)

Leaves, seeds and catkins
Sycamore (*Acer pseudoplatanus*)
English oak (*Quercus robur*)
Common beech (*Fagus sylvatica*)
Sweet chestnut (*Castanea sativa*)
Silver birch (*Betula pendula*)
Western hemlock (*Tsuga heterophylla*)

Holly-leaved cycad
(*Encephalartos ferox*)

Eurasian tree creepers
(*Certhia familiaris*)

Woodland flowers
Dog violet (*Viola riviniana*)
Crocus (*Crocus tommasinianus*)
Hepatica (*Anemone hepatica*)
Lily of the valley (*Convallaria majalis*)

Christmas Island red crab
(*Gecarcoidea natalis*)

Owston's palm civet
(*Chrotogale owstoni*)

Common raven (*Corvus corax*)

Eurasian hoopoe (*Upupa epops*)

Eucalyptus
Cider gum (*Eucalyptus gunnii*)

Yellow box eucalyptus
   (*Eucalyptus melliodora*)
Pink-flowered yellow gum
   (*Eucalyptus leucoxylon* 'Rosea')
Swamp gum (*Eucalyptus ovata*)
Silver-leaved mountain gum
   (*Eucalyptus pulverulenta*)
Great green bush cricket
   (*Tettigonia viridissima*)
Alpine newt (*Ichthyosaura
   alpestris*)
Ring-tailed lemur (*Lemur catta*)
Peacock tarantula
   (*Poecilotheria metallica*)
Sakura blossom (*Prunus serrulata*)
Western capercaillie
   (*Tetrao urogallus*)
Purple emperor butterfly
   (*Apatura iris*)
Pacarana (*Dinomys branickii*)
Saola (*Pseudoryx nghetinhensis*)
Eurasian lynx (*Lynx lynx*)
Fire salamander
   (*Salamandra salamandra*)
Elk (*Cervus canadensis*)
Cannonball tree
   (*Couroupita guianensis*)
Splendid leaf frog
   (*Cruziohyla calcarifer*)

Madagascar day gecko (*Phelsuma
   madagascariensis madagascariensis*)
Chinese water dragon
   (*Physignathus cocincinus*)
Pale green awlet (*Bibasis gomata*)
Guyana toucanet
   (*Selenidera piperivora*)
Feather-horned beetles
   (*Rhipicera femorata*)
European hedgehog
   (*Erinaceus europaeus*)
Red-bordered stink bugs
   (*Edessa rufomarginata*)
Trees
   Lombardy poplar
      (*Populus nigra* 'Italica')
   Scots pine (*Pinus sylvestris*)
   Philippine rosewood
      (*Petersianthus quadrialatus*)
   Elephant ear plant
      (*Colocasia esculenta*)
   Traveller's palm
      (*Ravenala madagascariensis*)
Striped skunk
   (*Mephitis mephitis*)
Bengal tiger (*Panthera tigris tigris*)
Broad-bordered bee hawk-moth
   (*Hemaris fuciformis*)
Eyed ladybug (*Anatis ocellata*)

Wild boar (*Sus scrofa*)
Wolf (*Canis lupus*)
Autograph tree seed pods
   (*Clusia rosea*)
Kakapo (*Strigops habroptilus*)
DeBrazza's monkey
   (*Cercopithecus neglectus*)
Palmer's chipmunk (*Tamias palmeri*)
Saucer magnolia
   (*Magnolia* x *soulangeana*) and
   long-tailed tits (*Aegithalos caudatus*)
Kirk's dik-dik (*Madoqua kirkii*)
Mushrooms and toadstools
   Fly agaric (*Amanita muscaria*)
   Glistening ink cap
      (*Coprinellus micaceus*)
   Wavy cap (*Psilocybe cyanescens*)
   Rosy bonnet (*Mycena rosea*)
   Witch's hat (*Hygrocybe conica*)
   Saffron milk cap (*Lactarius deliciosus*)
   Wood blewit (*Clitocybe nuda*)
   Honey fungus (*Armillaria mellea*)
   Shaggy ink cap (*Coprinus comatus*)
   Black trumpet
      (*Craterellus cornucopioides*)
Tree bumblebee (*Bombus hypnorum*)
Ruby-throated bulbul
   (*Pycnonotus dispar*) and cacao
   (*Theobroma cacao*)

Test your colour palettes and materials here...